Crumblers' Tea

Crumblers' Tea

Pandemic CellPhone Poems

Beata Ballard

CRUMBLERS' TEA
PANDEMIC CELLPHONE POEMS

iUniverse books may be ordered through booksellers or by contacting:

iUniverse
1663 Liberty Drive
Bloomington, IN 47403
www.iuniverse.com
844-349-9409

ISBN: 978-1-6632-3148-2 (sc)
ISBN: 978-1-6632-3149-9 (e)

Library of Congress Control Number: 2021922831

Print information available on the last page.

iUniverse rev. date: 04/27/2022

"Love, you are Love
Better far than a metaphor
Can ever, ever be…"

— The Fantasticks

To my Expanding Tribe
of Poets
and Ministering Earth-Angels

Contents

PART I

PART II

PART III

PART IV

PART V

PART VI

PART VII

PART I

"Enchanted cellphone in your trim blue-green"

Enchanted cellphone! In your trim blue-green
So tiny you fit snugly in my palm
Heard regularly, though at times unseen
Your presence acts upon me, like a balm
O caller to self-help in beams and bounds
In dark Pandemic Noon or night of care
In times of woe, your chime banal resounds
And rocks me in the knowledge that you're there
This evening, as I shelter in my room
And talk and text and exercise and pray
You're here, providing audio and Zoom
And real-time love close by and miles away
    Each sound-byte in a giggle, chirp or sigh
    That in an instant, could take wing and fly!

Prepercussions

A creature
fierce
and furious
has lately
broken free

and those
blithe fools
who put him
in his cage
(who could

they be?)
in lockdown
rage aloud
at their
transgression

Tomorrow
as they gaze
on greening
trees
and bluing sky

they'll think:
might we not
in the end
gain blessed
clemency?

Their walls
are
temporary
hence
they quake

(one cannot
know
what form
their punishment
will take)

To a Fastidious Reader

Yes, her poem
is sweet
yes, little

but you see
she's so
much more

Can you feel
your breathing
float her

off the page
down to
the floor?

Draw her
close, now
to the carpet

kiss she will
and warm
your toes

(sixteen
syllables still
to spring—

and bite
you, Reader
on the nose!)

"If intellect unleash awareness keen"

If intellect unleash awareness keen
And turn a poet's force to disarray
She'll languish on a past that might've been
Or cast strong doubts on doings of the day
If words strung on the page fail to entrance
She'll grumble 'gainst the colors of the light
Then rock the nether rhythms of romance
And chime in rhyme, in visions of the night
Eyes down, she'll let the darkness crack and roar
Let meanings deepen, let all logic cease
And she will feel her way to Heaven's Door
And note in her path onward, Love's increase
    At home at last, she'll credit for their part
    Love's Blinders, to ordain the poet's heart

PART II

Iowa Lockdown I

How happy you think
you'll be tomorrow or
some distant day
depends (I see it now)

upon your starting point
At present, how strange
and sweet to use
a novel simile

at the beginning of
the end of this
pandemic: you'll see!
Tonight, you'll miss

the touch of friends
yet bask in waves
of pleasure: your a/c's
kick and hum

your gem-like cellphone
screen, your neighbor's
reassuring feet that
softly tread the room

upstairs, lose yourself
inside the gentle creak
of boards that bend
'til in the warmth of Bliss

your load of cares
will reach an end:
"happy as a dead pig
in the sunshine"

Across the Pond

Her
Grace's
lawn
is
trod
upon

Her Grace's
grassy lawn is
trod, by four
overblown
guests

Her Grace's grassy
gusty sod is trod, by
four overblown guests
—with m a l l e t s

Ah, there they are—
the children!

They're playing tag
two limber lads, and
running alongside
a
hive
of
bees

Not quite at ease
she stands
and watches

She stands and watches
by the big bay window

What will
come next?

She
does
not
know

Crumblers' Tea

Like cinnamon
cake, love
I crumble for you

Come share it
with me, and I'll
pour the tea

and we'll kiss and
we'll dream if we
can't see the view

Come my fruitcake
still holding like glue
come to me

(ooh these nuts
how exciting— don't
mind if I do!)

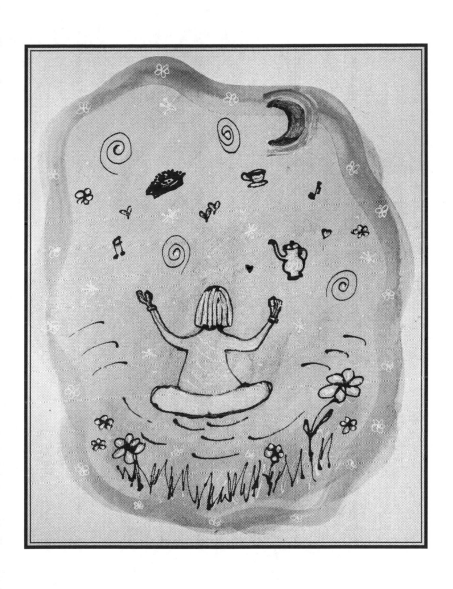

PART III

The Cake – a Tragicomedy

Oh, spare me the indignity
of a half-baked romance
the cake that I took out too soon
that didn't stand a chance

Did you preheat, he asks me
No, genius! It seemed hot
and I was in a hurry
while you, I guess, were not

So turn it on again, he says
And put the thing back in!
God help us, I am praying
lest I commit a sin.

I'm in my cups awaiting
and becoming very high
He's scrolling through his email
I watch him now and sigh

I'm so close to the oven
my face is turning red—
why not remove the cake, I think
and toss him in, instead!

Now don't go getting violent
—no need for him to die!
Just set the timer and take off—
let him eat cake! sez I —

Masked Cocktail

Tonight, I'll line
my legion
of illusions up
in ice-trays; I'll lay
them side by side

two trays
of fourteen cubes
each cube, a mask
each mask, a face
to talk to

Tonight, I will not
call them out
by name—that would
not do—but as
I think of one or two

of sometime-friends
in guise of ice
I'll pop them out
and plop them
in my glass

then, generously
I'll splash the tepid
liquid on their backs
the coke or rum
or vodka

taste and assess
then lightly trip
to living room
and nestle
in my sofa

and here, I think
I'll sip my drink
and ice will melt
and faces melt
and traces

of our places
(the blinders of
our days, now open
to the gentle rays
these too)

and he and she
and I and you
at rest at last
as one will melt
amen

What People Say

"What people say is usually
for their own benefit!"
These words were spoken
by my father
in softly-measured syllables
on the eve of Father's Day
some fifty years ago

Today, his meaning
springs up for review:
I think about
the cozy conversation
when his message
to his daughter
came out of the blue

Today
I know more
than that twenty-
something knew:
that my view
of my own benefit
changes as I grow

that listening to my father
not just to words
but to his pace
and to his pauses
in-between
was to my benefit
while gazing at his face

that since his heart was true
that my own benefit was his, too

Iowa Lockdown II

Today, *no hay problema*
if you're distancing again!
Be still, and listen long
enough—you'll savor much
of life: the steady rumba

of your upstairs neighbors'
naughty tumble-dryer
a breezy vacuum cleaner
pushed along not far
behind, but since you've

pressing work to do, you'll
sit up straighter in your chair
with the strong upholstered
back, reach for your laptop
log on in, scan through—

Hello! Two tiny feet above
your head come racing to
and fro! Old memories
flood in: a New York City
railroad flat, a five-year-old

half naked, wearing sneakers
climbs the walls, scares all
those entering—what fun to
be a tomboy—GET BACK
TO WORK, OLD LADY

The comic tribulations of a
French chef turning vegan
is the theme of this week's
story to translate, but now
as if on cue, you catch a whiff

of sweet corn floating down
then from beyond, a thump
a cry, a scraping chair, a lullaby
EARTH TO MADAM
COME BACK DOWN

Shouldn't you take a break?
The answer, as the French
say, is *pas evident;* still, there
is no sense getting soft, and
later, surely there'll be time

to lie in bed and listen to —
an owl? The wind? A floor-
board creak? What bliss!
Is life all this and Heaven too
—or Heaven and all this?

PART IV

"Shall I despair for you and me"

Shall I despair for you and me
Each in his rowboat, rowing
Against the current flowing
Who so alone will be?
Not I! For when you turn to see
My shallow strokes that flail in air
Your voice as true as prayer
Will rise, to guide us steadily
Oh cheer us onward, as we row
In unison, awake and strong
Felicity in tow!
Dive downward, angels! Play along
And charm the churlish wind below
And sing to it our song!

"There is an airy bond I am aware"

There is an airy bond I am aware
That hovers like a kite of double string
Wherein two runners, tugging here and there
Dart back and forth, to ease the fluttering
Aloft at last, an angel-bird will soar
Empowered by an all-embracing eye
Appearing now to be our guide on tour
To lead us on benignly from the sky
How gently and how gracefully it sways!
We watch it climb; the breezes 'round us still
It seems the culmination of my days
That joyfulness and silence now fulfill
    Ah but tomorrow, will it fly as well?
    Time and the kite, my friend, the tale will tell!

PART V

Birthday Song

I sing
the glory
of
a morning
ever
dawning

the
kindling
of
the rays
that spark
your day

If
I ask
How are you?
You know
I mean
to say

How
may
our voices
merge—
in what
sweet way?

If
my truth
provide
you comfort
I'm happy
as can be

and
if
your truth
in turn
provide
a haven

for
my truth—
then life
is one
near-perfect
rhapsody

Late-Pandemic Yogi

I've fallen off my mat!
(a gentle bump
of no more
than an inch
above the floor)

I'm sitting up
I'm looking 'round
I'm lying
back down
laughing

I feel the springy
soft caress of fresh
oatmeal-hued
carpet, on which
my fingers press

Here, fancy-free
my feelings fly
and one or two
or three
transgress

then melt inside
my inner eye
or seek
good-natured
to comply

and pass
through doors
whose hinges cry
(they'll open fully
by and by

or so
the wise
profess)

Lovely Old Lady

Lovely old lady
think back
to your start
harken
to words
that are true

On this wild
spinning globe
you're the green
you're the blue
you're the maiden
undying, my heart!

Open your ears
to the joy
and the pain
the dove
in deep mourning
the thrum of the rain

Open
your eyes
you are
what you see
the fluffiest cloud
the yellowest bee

Welcome
the puffs
of measured heat
embracing
your nose
and delicate feet

Lovely old lady
now, sigh
from your heart
nothing alive
is existing apart:
everything out there
is You!

"Thanksgiving on my own amounts to this"

Thanksgiving on my own amounts to this
A time to pause, to savor, to connect
With distant family, with friends I miss
To glimpse how diverse moons on each reflect
We reminisce as one, of yesterday
When we were son and daughter, girl and boy
And later through the years, of work and play
Recalling hopes and dreams and mutual joy
Our stories and travails in present time
We tell, the way we're meeting each demand
The pain, the unexpected bliss sublime
Encountering in the silence Love's own land
    Now from this distance, tripping forth anew
    Our thanks in bells come chiming, clear and true

PART VI

Midnight Surfer

Tonight, an angel face
this siren on her screen
will see, this media-

mermaid lost inside
her wandering
Tonight, two angel

wings will two hot
fins replace, to give
her flight; now watch

our Nereid flip
farewell, our former
surfer queen

now see her weep
in gratitude
and ease; now hear

her sing; now watch
as she leaps skyward
shimmering

demurring not
to glide in grace on
Heaven's gentle breeze

To My Heart

O Alchemist
My Heart
Atop Thy deck
mid fog of morn
I sound my horn

Enfolded now
inside the cold
this girl gone gray
O Heart, behold:
I bow and pray

On dull disaster's
brink, unsteady
on keel, I roll
yet land back
on my heel

As rope and rafter
shrink and creak
O Alchemist
My Heart
'tis Thee I seek!

"I'm most myself when reaching out to you"

I'm most myself when reaching out to you
I feel a tender blossoming in me
Here, in my innocence I am as true
As graceful as I ever hoped to be
Here, love's refreshing waters cool and clear
Well up within the stillness of my heart
I marvel at a source and course so near
A fountain dancing, showing off its art!
Contentment is my nature, to be sure
Though ne'er before so fluently expressed
Playful, exuberant, transparent, pure
Sparkling or soothing, captivating, blessed!
    In winter, love, if darts of fortune sting
    This Springtime shall I never cease to sing!

PART VII

"The world is our reflection, it is said"

The world is our reflection, it is said
My world appears a frothy muddled blue
In wavelets momentum thrusts ahead
To tumble to the shore of me and you
How pitiful that this should come to be!
We flounder on the surface, rolling blind
Our gaping rift now heaving restlessly
I ask, Have we left happiness behind?
But look! On land, we're sprinkling like rain!
See how we're forming rivers in the sand!
Could we, in love, a common course sustain
Each pledging to abide and understand?
    Out there are rainbows splashing in the sun
    Arising from the depths, they dance as one!

It's Here

It's here, it's here
at last, and it's
unblinkingly amused
a halo
'round a cloud
we recognize

It's come, it's come
today, with eyes
to see, and ears
to hear, and with
a heart that rocks
'til we capsize

The perfume
of approaching night
in every breath
we take
grows stronger
with each gust
as we set sail

Like shards
under a magnet
we cluster 'round
the dappled light
It's here, we're here
so frail, and yet —
so very bright!

Beata Ballard has worked with language all her life—as a writer and editor; as an instructor of French and Italian; and as a teacher of English-as-a-Second-Language (ESL). Her most satisfying accomplishment has been to facilitate nonnative pronunciation through "Jam Rap," a performance-based activity using rap-style monologues.

Her interest in writing poetry, which started in her teens, was revived through the use of her rhyming teaching materials.

A native of New York City, she received her early education in New York; Florence, Italy; and Aigle (Vaud), Switzerland. She earned her BS in languages (Russian) from Georgetown University's Faculty of Languages and Linguistics, and her MA-TESL from Saint Michael's College.

Past areas of work and residence include New York, NY; San Francisco, CA; Chapel Hill and Durham, NC; West Palm Beach, FL; Rome, Italy; and Dakar, Senegal, West Africa. She recently moved back to Fairfield, Iowa, home of Maharishi International University, where she taught ESL in the Nineties.

This is her second chapbook of poetry.

Printed in the United States
by Baker & Taylor Publisher Services